This book belongs to

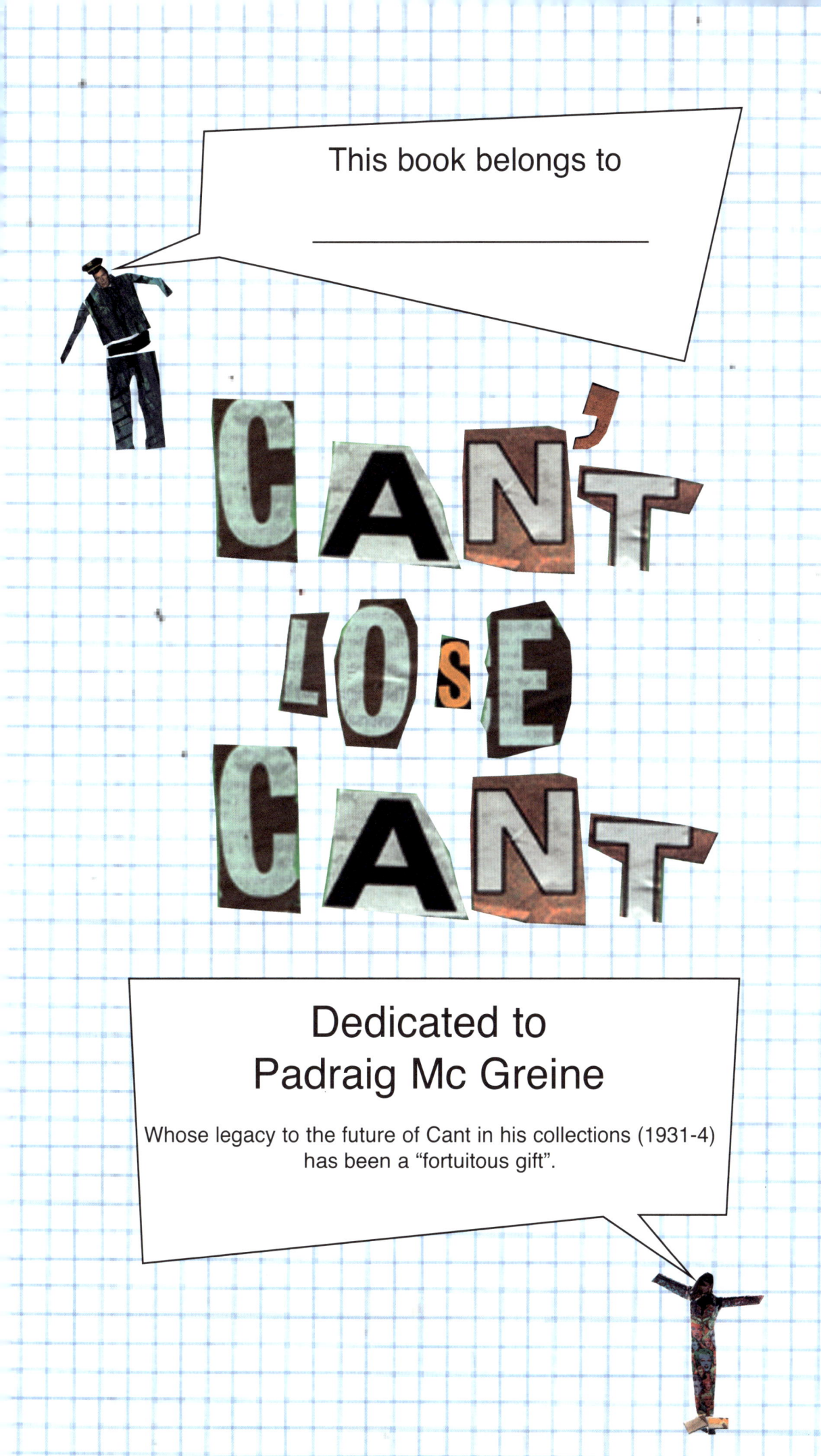

_____

CANT LOSE CANT

Dedicated to
Padraig Mc Greine

Whose legacy to the future of Cant in his collections (1931-4) has been a "fortuitous gift".

Cant [kant]

Today Cant is a vocabulary spoken in an English grammatical structure. This means the book is very easy to use. The following guidelines will be helpful to build a repertoire of Cant phrases and sentences for the adult or the child learning Cant.

1. Start with one Cant word in a sentence;

    I see the lakín. [I see the girl.]

2. Then use two Cant words in a sentence;

    The lakín is in the gruppa. [The girl is in the shop.]

3. Cant verbs have the same endings as English verbs;

    He glórchs. [He looks.] He glorched. [He looked.] He is glorching. [He is looking.]

    The súbla glórched at the corraí. [The boy looked at the horse.]

4. Adjectives in Cant follow the same order as English;
    Biní claudóg [Small hen]
    The biní claudóg boged me a rúmóg. [The small hen gave me an egg.]

5. Ask questions in Cant;
    Where is the tóm corraí? [Where is the big horse?]
    The tóm corraí is in the sark. [The big horse is in the field.]

6. Use Cloze exercises;
    The feen is táiring to the _____. [The boy is talking to the _____.]
            lakin   alamach   dora   [girl   milk   bread]

7. Tell a story in Cant;
    The lakín missled to the gruppa [The girl went to the shop]
    She boged some dora. [She got some bread.]
    She gave the feen gairéad. [She gave the man money.]
    When she missled home she put aid on the dora and she lushed it.
    [When she went home she put butter on the bread and she ate it.]

Using the glossary;
    The Cant word is followed by the Irish then the English translation.
    [:] signifies a long vowel; [a: ball] [e: plate] [i: meat] [o: go] [u: tube]

As Ireland embraces a new intercultural identity at the start of the second millennium, we must remember that the Traveller community, as Ireland's indigenous minority group, is an important part of intercultural Ireland. This book focuses on one language, Cant, but it also provides a valuable model for discussing the range of language and dialect variety in our schools today. We hope teachers and other professionals will use it as a starting point for raising awareness of language diversity. It shows how making a book can raise the status of a language in the classroom. It offers children the opportunity to become teachers to their peers, and experience the power of learning through creative activity. The model of working exemplified in this book places the emphasis on collaborative learning. In this way children make links between languages thus supporting a development education approach in the classroom. This book is part of a new series of books from Kids' Own Publishing Partnership called 'Unheard Voices'.

súbla [su:bla]	lakín [laki:n]
buachaill 	cailín 
boy	girl

feen [fi:n]	beoir [bo:r]
fear 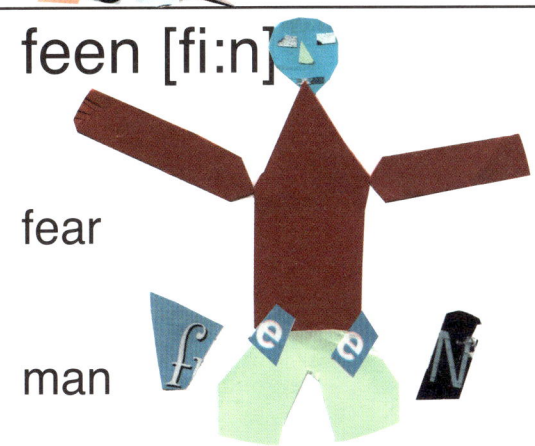	bean 
man	woman

gathera [gathera]	naderum [naderum]
athair 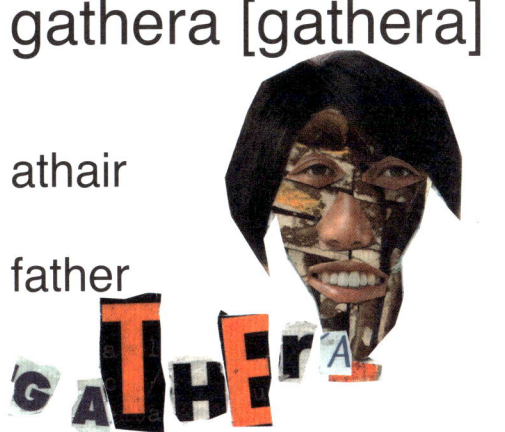	máthair 
father	mother

nídes [ni:djes]

daoine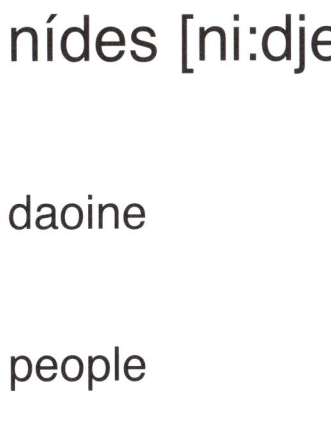

people

| Glórch [glo:rk] | feach | look |

midil [midil]

diabhal

devil

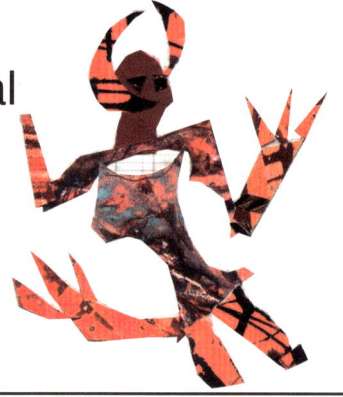

Dhaluin [galu:n]

Dia

God

glochlai [glo:klai]

múinteoir

teacher

cuinne [ku:nye]

sagart

priest

séideog [she:do:g]

garda

guard

goyas [go:yas]

leanaí

children

| táirí [ta:ri] | labhaír | speak |

blánóg [bla:no:g]	bleater [bli:ter]
bó	caora
cow	sheep

claudóg [klaudo:g]	lapróg [lapro:g]
cearc	lacha
hen	duck

comera [komera]	creeper [kri:per]
madra	cait
dog	cat

múóg [mu:o:g]	corraí [kori:]
muc	capall
pig	horse

missel [misl]	tóm [to:m]	biní [bini:]
teigh	mór	beag
go	big	little

dora [dora]

arán

bread

aid [aid]

im

butter

cullens [kulenz]

prátaí

potatoes

fe [fe:]

feoil

meat

innocknibs [inokni:bz]

tornapaí

turnips

alamach [alamak]

bainne

milk

muggels [mugls]

úlla

apples

scoi chelpí [skai chelpi:]

tae

tea

---

bog [bog]

tabhair

give

lush [lush]

ith/ól

eat/drink

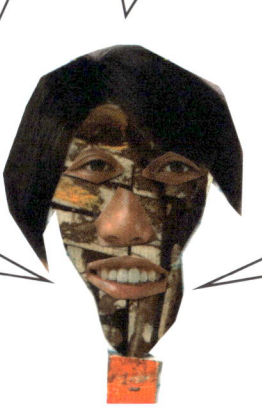

Scoi chelpí, dora and **aid**

Altamach

What do you lush for your breakfast?

I lush scoi chelpí, dora and aid for my breakfast.

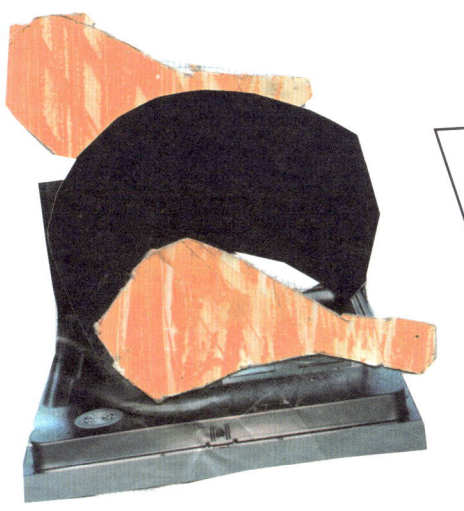

What happened to the cullen who refused to work?

He got the chop!

céna [ke:na] teach house 	**grépéil [gre:pe:l]** seipeal church
gruppa [grupa] siopa shop 	**rispún [rispu:n]**  príosún jail
rudas [rudas] doras door 	**grinóg [grino:g]**  fuinneog window
sráta [shra:ta] geata gate 	**lorc [lork]** carr car

cherra [chera]

tine

fire

lúbán [lu:ba:n]

puball

tent

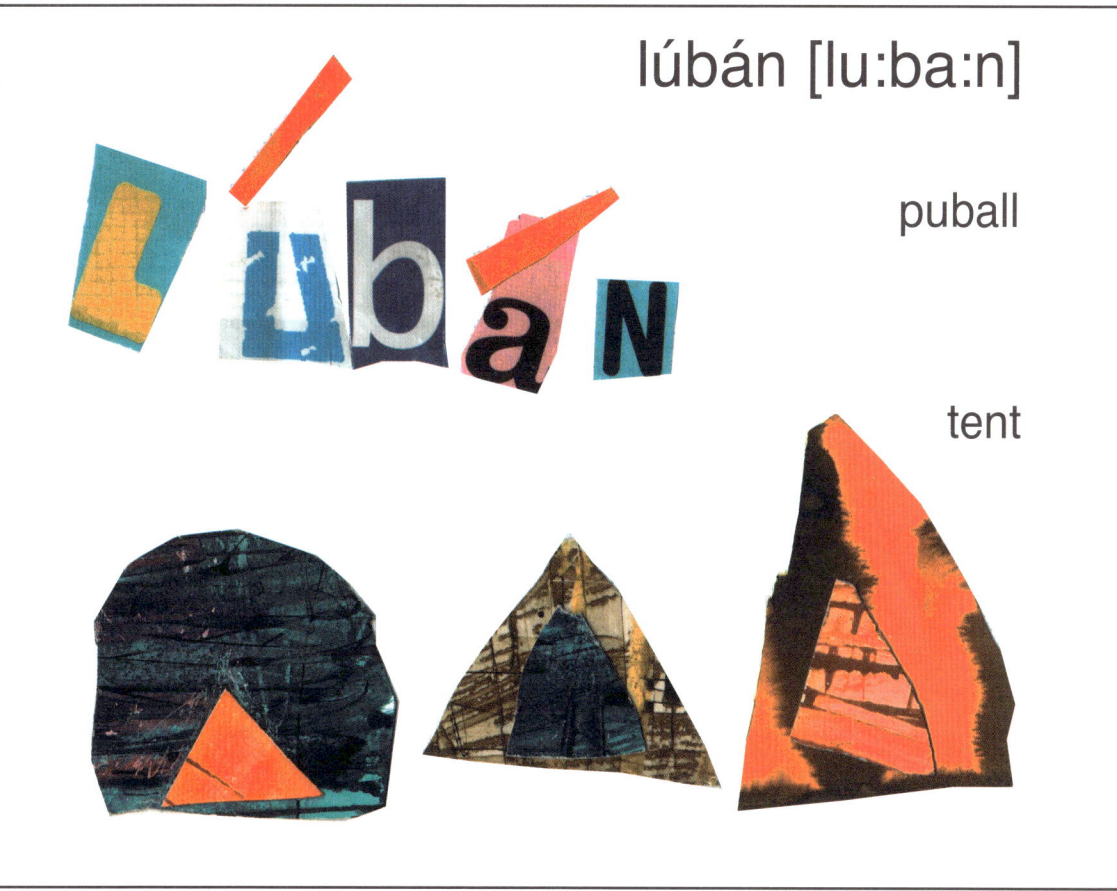

gup [gup] fuar cold

"Light the cherra because we are gup in our lúbán."

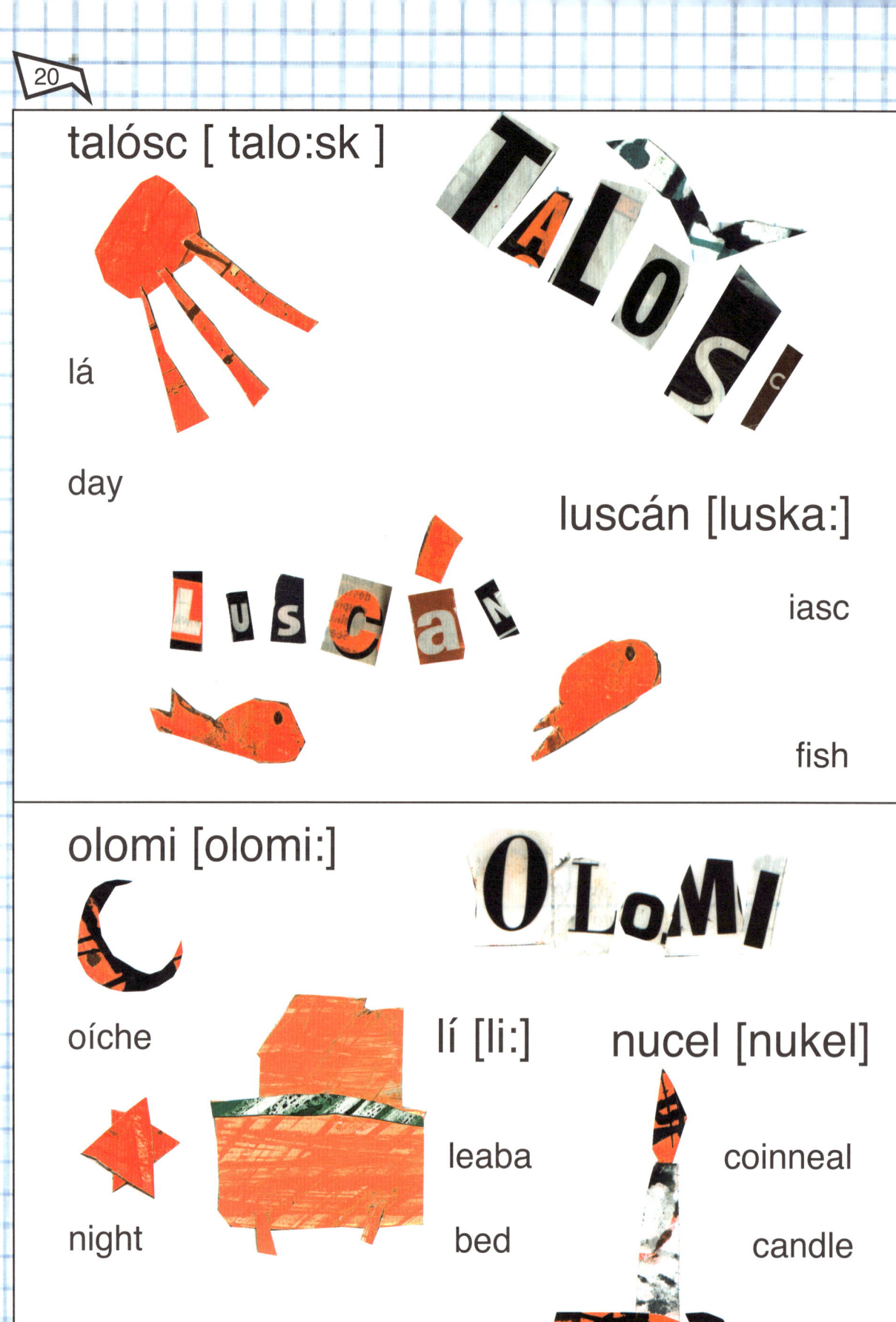

talósc [talo:sk]

lá

day

luscán [luska:]

iasc

fish

olomi [olomi:]

oíche

night

lí [li:]

leaba

bed

nucel [nukel]

coinneal

candle

reeb [ri:b] gruaig hair 	**lúrógs** [lu:ro:gs] súiles eyes 
pí [pí:] béal mouth 	**máilles** [ma:les] lámha hands 
griffin [grifin] cóta coat 	**tugs** [tugz] eadaí clothes 
guillimins [guili:mi:nz] bróga shoes 	**ríspa** [rispa] bríste trousers 

If you want to make pictures like the ones in this book you'll need some old magazines, some card, paint, scissors, glue and paper.

Colour the plain card with different colours. Then cut the coloured card into interesting shapes. We made collages combining the coloured card and pictures from magazines.

Try It!